MW00578677

Published by Barbour Publishing, Inc., P.O. Box 719, Uhrichsville, Ohio 44683
http://www.barbourbooks.com

 Member of the
Evangelical Christian
Publishers Association

Printed in the United States of America.

GOD BLESS AMERICA

RACHEL QUILLIN

BARBOUR
PUBLISHING, INC.
Uhrichsville, Ohio

God, You've blessed America
With riches beyond compare—
Golden fields, glorious skies—
So many beauties rare.

You've given us great freedom
And smiled upon this land,
As our fathers walked beside You
And followed Your commands.

Now, Father, give us wisdom
To walk with You once more,
So You can bless this nation
As You have done before.

RACHEL QUILLIN

TABLE OF CONTENTS

INTRODUCTION

God has blessed this nation from its birth. In the beginning, He allowed our founding fathers to settle here as they escaped religious bondage. Their desire was to worship Him in the way that they believed the Bible commanded them to. When they began to establish our government, they sought God's guidance, and He blessed them beyond measure.

Today we are still reaping the blessings that are a result of our forefathers' obedience to God. We have freedoms that many nations do not enjoy. We have a beautiful land that yields bountiful harvests, and we enjoy riches that exceed our needs. We receive educations that those in many nations can only dream about.

Without a doubt, the greatest gift God still grants us is the freedom to worship Him the way that the Bible tells us to. It is my prayer that this book will be a reminder of the blessings of God in the past and an encouragement to us to live in a way that will allow Him to bless us in the future.

Righteousness exalteth a nation: but sin is a reproach to any people.
PROVERBS 14:34

1

GOD BLESS AMERICA

And all these blessings shall come on thee, and overtake thee,
if thou shalt hearken unto the voice of the LORD thy God.

DEUTERONOMY 28:2

Freedom is not a gift bestowed upon us by other men, but a right that belongs to us by the laws of God and nature. . . . I never doubted the existence of the Deity, that He made the world and governed it by His Providence. . . . The pleasures of this world are rather from God's goodness than our own merit. . . . Whoever shall introduce into the public affairs the principles of primitive Christianity will change the face of the world.

BENJAMIN FRANKLIN

Let our object be our country, our whole country, and nothing but our country. And, by the blessing of God, may that country itself become a vast and splendid monument, not of oppression and terror, but of wisdom, of peace, and of liberty, upon which the world may gaze with admiration forever.

DANIEL WEBSTER

Father, thank You for Your abundant blessings on this great nation.
Please help us to daily remember them
and to never take them for granted.

I will make of thee a great nation,
and I will bless thee,
and make thy name great.

2

AMERICA'S GREATNESS

*The LORD shall command the blessing upon thee in thy storehouses,
and in all that thou settest thine hand unto; and he shall bless thee
in the land which the LORD thy God giveth thee.*
DEUTERONOMY 28:8

A great people has been moved to defend a great nation. Terrorist attacks can shake the foundations of our biggest buildings, but they cannot touch the foundation of America. These acts shattered steel, but they cannot dent the steel of American resolve.

America was targeted for attack because we're the brightest beacon for freedom and opportunity in the world. And no one will keep that light from shining. . . .

None of us will ever forget this day.

Yet, we go forward to defend freedom and all that is good and just in our world.

. . .God bless America.

» GEORGE W. BUSH »

A general dissolution of principles and manners will more surely overthrow the liberties of America than the whole force of the common enemy. While the people are virtuous they cannot be subdued; but when once they lose their virtue they will be ready to surrender their liberties to the first external or internal invader. . . . If virtue and knowledge are diffused among the people, they will never be enslaved. This will be their great security.

SAMUEL ADAMS

I sought for the greatness and the genius of America in her ample rivers—it was not there; in her fertile fields and boundless prairies, and it was not there; in her rich mines and her vast world commerce, and it was not there. Not until I went into the churches of America and heard her pulpits ablaze with righteousness did I meet the secret of her genius and power. America is great because she is good, and if America ever ceases to be good, America will cease to be great.

ALEXIS DE TOCQUEVILLE

The New Colossus

Not like the brazen giant of Greek fame,
With conquering limbs astride from land to land;
Here at the sea-washed, sunset gates shall stand
A mighty woman with a torch, whose flame
Is the imprisoned lightning, and her name
Mother of Exiles. From her beacon-hand
Glows worldwide welcome; her mild eyes command
The air-bridged harbor that twin cities frame.
"Keep ancient lands, your storied pomp!" cries she
With silent lips. "Give me your tired, your poor,
Your huddled masses yearning to breathe free,
The wretched refuse of your teeming shore.
Send these, the homeless, tempest-tossed, to me,
I lift my lamp beside the golden door!"

EMMA LAZARUS

The poet called Miss Liberty's torch, "the lamp beside the golden door." Well, that was the entrance to America, and it still is. . . .

The glistening hope of that lamp is still ours. Every promise, every opportunity is still golden in this land. And through that golden door our children can walk into tomorrow with the knowledge that no one can be denied the promise that is America.

Her heart is full; her torch is still golden, her future bright. She has arms big enough to comfort and strong enough to support, for the strength in her arms is the strength of her people. She will carry on . . .unafraid, unashamed, and unsurpassed.

" RONALD REAGAN "

A nation is formed by the willingness of each of us to share in the responsibility for upholding the common good.

BARBARA JORDAN

Here is not merely a nation but a teeming nation of nations.

WALT WHITMAN

We shall not fight alone. God presides over the destinies of nations and will raise up friends for us. The battle is not to the strong alone; it is to the vigilant, the active, the brave! . . . I know not what course others may take, but as for me, give me liberty or give me death!

"PATRICK HENRY"

The past few days when I've been at that window upstairs, I've thought a bit of the "shining city upon a hill." The phrase comes from John Winthrop, who wrote it to describe the America he imagined. What he imagined was important because he was an early Pilgrim, an early freedom man. He journeyed here on what today we'd call a little wooden boat; and like the other Pilgrims, he was looking for a home that would be free.

I've spoken of the shining city all my political life, but I don't know if I ever quite communicated what I saw when I said it. But in my mind it was a tall, proud city built on rocks stronger than oceans, windswept, God-blessed, and teeming with people of all kinds living in harmony and peace; a city with free ports that hummed with commerce and creativity. And if there had to be city walls, the walls had doors, and the doors were open to anyone with the will and the heart to get here. That's how I saw it, and see it still. . . . And so. . . , God bless you, and God bless the United States of America.

' RONALD REAGAN'

Neither the wisest constitution nor the wisest laws will secure the liberty and happiness of a people whose manners are universally corrupt. He therefore is the truest friend of the liberty of his country who tries most to promote its virtue, and who, so far as his power and influence extend, will not suffer a man to be chosen into any office of power and trust who is not a wise and virtuous man.

SAMUEL ADAMS

It cannot be emphasized too strongly or too often that this great
nation was founded, not by religionists, but by Christians;
not on religions, but on the gospel of Jesus Christ.
For this very reason peoples of other faiths
have been afforded asylum, prosperity,
and freedom of worship here.

PATRICK HENRY

Dear God, it is only by Your mercy that America is great.
She's a land of opportunity and freedom because
You've chosen to bless her.
Thank You, Jesus, for Your goodness.

The LORD bless thee, and keep thee:
The LORD make his face shine upon thee,
and be gracious unto thee.

NUMBERS 6:24–25

3

GOD'S WISDOM FOR OUR NATION

The LORD shall greatly bless thee in the land which the LORD thy God giveth thee. . . . Only if thou carefully hearken unto the voice of the LORD thy God, to observe to do all these commandments which I command thee this day.

DEUTERONOMY 15:4–5

The highest glory of the American Revolution was this;
it connected in one indissoluble bond the principles of
civil government with the principles of Christianity. From
the day of the Declaration. . .they [the American people]
were bound by the laws of God, which they all, and by
the laws of the gospel, which they nearly all, acknowledge
as the rules of their conduct.

JOHN QUINCY ADAMS

You have rights antecedent to all earthly governments; rights that cannot be repealed or restrained by human laws; rights derived from the Great Legislator of the Universe.

JOHN ADAMS

Belief in and dependence on God is absolutely essential.
It will be an integral part of our public life as long as I am governor.

RONALD REAGAN

In this situation of this assembly, groping, as it were, in the dark to find political truth. . .how has it happened, sir, that we have not hitherto once thought of humbly applying to the Father of lights to illuminate our understandings? In the beginning of the contest with Britain, when we were sensible of danger, we had daily prayers in this room for the divine protection. Our prayers, sir, were heard; they were graciously answered. . . . Have we now forgotten that powerful Friend?

I have lived, sir, a long time; and the longer I live, the more convincing proofs I see of this truth, that God governs in the affairs of men. And if a sparrow cannot fall to the ground without His notice, is it probable that an empire can rise without His aid? We have been assured, sir, in the sacred writings, that "except the LORD build the house, they labor in vain that build it." I firmly believe this; and I also believe, that without His concurring aid, we shall succeed in this political building no better than the builders of Babel; we shall be divided by our little, partial, local interests, our projects will be confounded, and we ourselves shall become a reproach and a byword to future ages.

BENJAMIN FRANKLIN

We have staked the whole future of American civilization, not upon the power of government, far from it. We have staked the future of all of our political institutions upon the capacity of each and all of us to govern ourselves, to control ourselves, to sustain ourselves according to the Ten Commandments of God.

JAMES MADISON

The God who gave us life gave us liberty. And can the liberties of a nation be thought secure when we have removed their only firm basis, a conviction in the minds of the people that these liberties are of the gift of God? That they are not to be violated but with His wrath? Indeed, I tremble for my country when I reflect that God is just; that His justice cannot sleep forever.

THOMAS JEFFERSON

Liberty cannot be established without morality, nor morality without faith.

HORACE GREELY

Providence has given our people the choice of their rulers,
and it is the duty as well as the privilege
and interest of our Christian nation
to select and prefer Christians for their rulers.

JOHN JAY

Blessed is the nation whose God is the LORD; and the people whom he hath chosen for his own inheritance.

PSALM 33:12

It is the duty of nations, as well as of men,
to own their dependence upon the overruling power of God
and to recognize the sublime truth announced in the Holy Scriptures
and proven by all history, that those nations only
are blessed whose God is the Lord.

ABRAHAM LINCOLN

God is going to reveal to us things he never revealed before if we put our hands in His. No books ever go into my laboratory. The thing I am to do and the way of doing it are revealed to me. I never have to grope for methods. The method is revealed to me the moment I am inspired to create something new. Without God to draw aside the curtain I would be helpless.

GEORGE WASHINGTON CARVER

$God's$ signs are not always the ones we look for. We learn in tragedy that his purposes are not always our own. Yet the prayers of private suffering, whether in our homes or in this great cathedral, are known and heard and understood. . . .

America is a nation full of good fortune, with so much to be grateful for. But we are not spared from suffering. In every generation, the world has produced enemies of human freedom. They have attacked America, because we are freedom's home and defender. And the commitment of our fathers is now the calling of our time.

On this national day of prayer and remembrance, we ask almighty God to watch over our nation, and grant us patience and resolve in all that is to come. We pray that He will comfort and console those who now walk in sorrow. We thank Him for each life we now must mourn and the promise of a life to come.

As we have been assured, neither death nor life, nor angels nor principalities nor powers, nor things present nor things to come, nor height, nor depth, can separate us from God's love. May He bless the souls of the departed. May He comfort our own. And may He always guide our country.

God bless America.

GEORGE W. BUSH

We have been the recipients of the choicest bounties of Heaven. We have been preserved these many years in peace and prosperity. We have grown in numbers, wealth, and power as no other nation has ever grown. But we have forgotten God. . . . We have vainly imagined, in the deceitfulness of our hearts, that all these blessings were produced by some superior wisdom and virtue of our own. Intoxicated with unbroken success, we have become too self-sufficient to feel the necessity of redeeming and preserving grace, too proud to pray to the God that made us!

ABRAHAM LINCOLN

The moral principles and precepts contained in the Scriptures ought to form the basis of all our civil constitutions and laws. All the miseries and evils which men suffer from vice, crime, ambition, injustice, oppression, slavery and war, proceed from their despising or neglecting the precepts contained in the Bible.

NOAH WEBSTER

$\mathcal{All}$ the good from the Savior of the world is communicated through this Book [the Bible]; but for the Book we could not know right from wrong. All the things desirable to man are contained in it.

ABRAHAM LINCOLN

What a sad condition would the world be in without gospel light! All places would be dens of rapine, and mountains of prey. Certainly we owe much of our civil liberty, and outward tranquillity to gospel light. If a sword, or variance, at any time, follow the gospel, it is but an accidental, not a direct and proper effect of it.

JOHN FLAVEL

It would be peculiarly improper to omit, in this first official act, my fervent supplication to that almighty being, who rules over the universe, who presides in the councils of nations, and whose providential aids can supply every human defect, that His benediction may consecrate to the liberties and happiness of the people of the United States. . . . No people can be bound to acknowledge and adore the invisible hand which conducts the affairs of men more than the people of the United States. Every step by which they have advanced to the character of an independent nation seems to have been distinguished by some token of providential agency. . . . We ought to be no less persuaded that the propitious smiles of heaven can never be expected on a nation that disregards the eternal rules of order and right, which heaven itself has ordained.

GEORGE WASHINGTON

"Oh Lord, we are proud to be Americans.
Help us to be prouder still to be Christians.
Help us to seek Your face
and follow Your ways,
for we know that then Your blessing
will be upon us."

If my people, which are called by my name,
shall humble themselves,
and pray, and seek my face,
and turn from their wicked ways;
then will I hear from heaven,
and will forgive their sin,
and will heal their land.

2 CHRONICLES 7:14